THE BRITANNICA COMMON CORE LIBRARY

# WHAT IS
# NONFICTION?

JEANNE NAGLE

**Britannica**
Educational Publishing

IN ASSOCIATION WITH

# ROSEN
EDUCATIONAL SERVICES

Published in 2015 by Britannica Educational Publishing (a trademark of Encyclopædia Britannica, Inc.) in association with The Rosen Publishing Group, Inc.
29 East 21st Street, New York, NY 10010

Distributed exclusively by Rosen Publishing.
To see additional Britannica Educational Publishing titles, go to rosenpublishing.com.

First Edition

**Britannica Educational Publishing**
J. E. Luebering: Director, Core Reference Group
Mary Rose McCudden: Editor, Britannica Student Encyclopedia

**Rosen Publishing**
Hope Lourie Killcoyne: Executive Editor
Nelson Sá: Art Director
Brian Garvey: Designer
Cindy Reiman: Photography Manager

**Library of Congress Cataloging-in-Publication Data**

Nagle, Jeanne, author.
What is Nonfiction?/Jeanne Nagle. – First Edition.
        pages cm. — (The Britannica Common Core Library)
Includes bibliographical references and index.
ISBN 978-1-62275-656-8 (library bound) — ISBN 978-1-62275-657-5 (pbk.) — ISBN 978-1-62275-658-2 (6-pack)
1. Literary form—Juvenile literature. 2. Prose literature—Juvenile literature. I. Title.
PN45.5.N34 2015
808—dc23
                                                                            2014023022

*Manufactured in the United States of America*

*Cover (background) © iStockphoto.com/marcoventuriniautieri; cover (hands and tablet) © iStockphoto.com/Anatoliy Babiy; cover (tablet screen), pp. 21, 23 © Rosen Publishing; p. 1, interior pages background image © iStockphoto.com/ytwong; p. 4 DEA/G. Dagli Orti/De Agostini/Getty Images; pp. 5, 19 © AP Images; p. 6 RimDream/Shutterstock.com; p. 7 Charles Maraia/Taxi/Getty Images; p 9 © Michael Newman/PhotoEdit; p. 10 Culture Club/Hulton Archive/Getty Images; p. 12 Rita Kochmarjova/Shutterstock.com; p. 13 Tetra Images/Erik Isakson/Brand X Pictures/Getty Images; p. 14 Hulton Archive/Getty Images; p. 15 Gamma-Rapho/Getty Images; pp. 16, 22, 24 Library of Congress Prints and Photographs Division; p. 17 Private Collection/Photo © Christie's Images/Bridgeman Images; p. 18 Dougal Waters/Photodisc/Getty Images; p. 20 Joe Raedle/Getty Images; p. 25 Kean Collection/Archive Photos/Getty Images; p. 26 DEA/M. Seemuller/De Agostini/Getty Images; p. 27 Courtesy Groundwood Books; p. 28 Trombax/Shutterstock.com; p. 29 Mario Tama/Getty Images.*

# What Is Nonfiction?

People have been writing down stories for thousands of years. A story may be written to entertain readers, to inform readers, or to do both of these things. Most stories are told using a type of ordinary writing called **prose**.

There are two main types of prose: fiction and

Writing that presents facts or true events is called nonfiction.

nonfiction. Fiction, such as novels and short stories, is mostly made up. Nonfiction, such as histories, speeches, and letters, is not made up. It presents facts and ideas about real events and people.

The purpose of nonfiction is to record and share information. Nonfiction is often entertaining, too. Some well-known writers of nonfiction for children include Russell Freedman, Shelley Tanaka, and Gary Paulsen.

Gary Paulsen's nonfiction book Woodsong *describes his adventures training for and racing in an 1,100-mile (1,770-kilometer) dogsled race across Alaska. The race is known as the Iditarod.*

# Types of Nonfiction

There are many types of nonfiction prose. Some popular forms include essays, reports, biographies, journals, histories, and speeches.

## Essays

An essay is a short piece of writing in which the writer shares his or her views on a subject. Essays usually have **opinions** in them, and they speak directly to the reader.

## Reports

Reports are written to describe how or why things happen. A report may also explain what something is

*Students write many nonfiction reports and essays for school.*

or how it works. A science report contains many more facts than opinions. Other kinds, such as a book report, may include more opinions.

An **opinion** is a belief based on facts but is not necessarily the truth. An opinion shows what a person feels or thinks about something.

## Biographies

A biography tells the story of a real person's life. Biographies are not written by the people they are about. When someone writes about his or her own life, it is called an autobiography.

You can find interesting facts about real people in biographies.

7

## Journals and Diaries

A journal, or diary, is a record of the day-to-day events in a person's life. Often the writer describes his or her ideas and feelings about experiences. Journals can help people understand what life was like in the past.

## Histories

Histories are records of the past. Biographies, autobiographies, journals, letters, speeches, and some kinds of reports

*A writer often puts private thoughts and feelings in a diary.*

are all forms of history. Another broader form of history discusses the events within communities, or **societies**. A history may discuss a particular event or it may tell about many events and people related to a society.

*Books that contain speeches help us learn about the leaders who delivered those speeches.*

## Speeches

Speeches are written for a specific audience. They are usually meant to persuade people to think or do something. Many famous speeches are now read as nonfiction prose.

**Societies** are groups of people living at particular times and places.

# Nonfiction in Action

The following examples model different forms of nonfiction.

## Thoughts and Feelings: Example of an Essay

Famous children's author Louisa May Alcott

Louisa May Alcott started writing at a young age. She published many types of fiction and nonfiction. As an adult, she supported her family with her writing. She is best known for her fiction novel Little Women.

once worked as a servant. She wrote an essay about her experiences called "How I Went Out to Service" (1874). She begins by explaining her situation:

> When I was eighteen I wanted something to do. I had tried teaching for two years, and hated it; I had tried sewing, and could not earn my bread in that way, at the cost of health; I tried story-writing and got five dollars for stories which now bring a hundred; I had thought seriously of going upon the stage . . .
>
> "What shall I do?" was still the question that **perplexed** me. I was ready to work . . . But the right task seemed hard to find . . .

To be **perplexed** is to be uncertain or confused.

## A Study Shared: Example of a Report

The famous scientist Charles Darwin wrote a report on how animals express feelings. This passage is from *The Expression of Emotion in Man and Animals* (1872).

*In his report, Darwin describes what he has noticed about dog behavior.*

*Dogs, when approaching a strange dog, may find it useful to show by their movements that they are friendly, and do not wish to fight. When two young dogs in play are growling and biting each other's faces and legs, it is obvious that they . . . understand each other's gestures and manners. There seems, indeed, some degree of* **instinctive** *knowledge in puppies and kittens, that they must not use their sharp little teeth or claws too freely in their play . . .*

**Instinctive** knowledge comes naturally or automatically.

## Nonfiction Writers

Some nonfiction books are like "how-to reports," such as Baseball Lessons: How to Pitch, written by baseball coach Steve Adler.

## Let's Compare

The difference between an essay and a report is that an essay has more opinions than facts. A report normally has more facts than opinions.

Louisa May Alcott's essay uses words like "wanted," "hated," "tried," and "perplexed" to show how she feels about not having work. Her essay describes facts about her situation. However, Alcott's main point behind those facts is how she feels about not being able to find the right job.

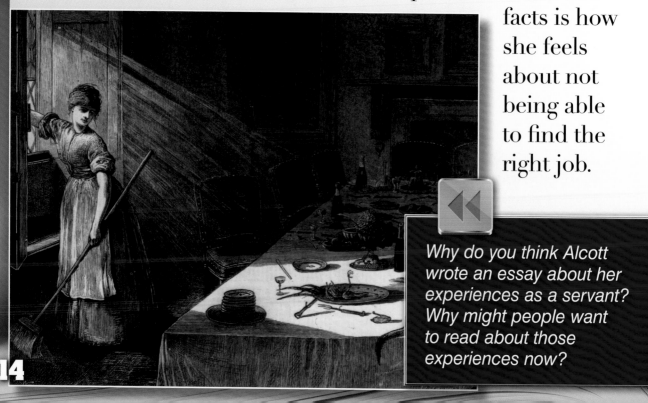

*Why do you think Alcott wrote an essay about her experiences as a servant? Why might people want to read about those experiences now?*

*Why might people today want to read Darwin's report on the feelings of animals?*

Charles Darwin, on the other hand, reports about the feelings animals experience and express. Darwin discusses feelings based on what he has seen, rather than what he believes. He uses words like "it is obvious" and "there seems" to show that he is not reporting opinions but events he has **observed** during his study of animals.

**Observed** means noticed or watched carefully.

## A Childhood Story: Example of an Autobiography

In 1902, Charles A. Eastman finished a **memoir** about his childhood in a Native American community called *Indian Boyhood*. Following are passages from that work.

A **memoir** is a kind of autobiography, but it usually covers only certain memories, rather than a writer's whole life.

Charles A. Eastman attended Dartmouth College and earned a degree in medicine from Boston University. He wrote a number of books to educate people about Native American customs and beliefs.

The Indian boy was a prince of the wilderness. He had but very little work to do during the period of his boyhood. His principal occupation was the practice of a few simple arts in warfare and the chase. Aside from this, he was master of his time.

Whatever was required of us boys was quickly performed: then the field was clear for our games and plays. There was always keen competition among us. We felt very much as our fathers did in hunting and war . . .

Eastman's story paints a clear picture of Indian life.

## Shared Secrets:
## Example of a Diary or Journal

A girl named Rita kept a diary while living in Austria in the early 1900s. *A Young Girl's Diary* was later printed in English in 1921. In this passage, Rita writes about sharing her diary with a friend.

*Writers usually use diaries to record their private thoughts. Why do you think Rita shares her diary with Hella?*

*We write on loose pages. Hella thinks it's better because then one does not have to tear anything out. But we have promised one another to throw nothing away and not to tear anything up. Why should we? One can tell a friend everything. A pretty friend if one couldn't.*

## Nonfiction Writers

During World War II, a young Jewish girl, Anne Frank, kept a diary for two years while hiding from the Nazis with her family. From the diary, readers have found out what Jewish people experienced and felt during that time.

## Let's Compare

Diaries and journals are not as strict in the way they present information as biographies and autobiographies are. They are also more personal than autobiographies. This is because they are usually not written for the public.

*Steve Jobs by Walter Isaacson*

*Steve Jobs was one of the founders of Apple Inc., one of the most successful companies in the world. Many people want to read his biography.*

In *A Young Girl's Diary*, Rita writes, "One can tell a friend everything." She mentions that she and Hella write on "loose pages" and that they will "throw nothing away." Two friends share a promise about a diary. However, their diary is not meant for others to read.

In *Indian Boyhood*, Eastman describes his boyhood as an adult would or as the public he writes for might think about it. He says the Indian boy is "a prince of the wilderness." Words like "work," "competition," and "master" help the public understand his boyhood. Eastman's personal thoughts as a boy are not the main point of his writing.

LEADING WOMEN

Teenage Education Activist Who Defied the Taliban

*Malala Yousafzai*

CATHLEEN SMALL

Malala Yousafzai protested the closing of girls' schools in her area. She was shot because of her protests. Her bravery inspired the world. Biographies continue to be written about her.

## A Design from Long Ago: Example of a History

In 1896, Sarah E. Champion wrote *Our Flag*, a history of the American flag. This passage describes how Betsy Ross met with George Washington to discuss the flag's design before she made it:

Nonfiction writing can bring moments in history to life.

. . . Washington drew with a pencil a design for her to follow.

There is no doubt but that she made the first flag and that she made them for the government for several years.

It is said that Washington drew his stars with six points . . . but that Mrs. Ross changed it to the five-pointed shape . . . Our flags always have the five-pointed stars, our coins the six-pointed.

## Nonfiction Writers

Jane Yolen wrote two history books for children about female pirates: *Pirates in Petticoats* (1963) and *Sea Queens: Women Pirates Around the World* (2008).

About the Author
Meet
Jane Yolen
Alice B. McGinty

## From President Lincoln: Example of a Speech

Abraham Lincoln delivered the Gettysburg Address in 1863 to honor soldiers lost in the battle of Gettysburg. The battle had turned the tide of the American Civil War in favor of the Union. On the adjacent page, the president reminds his audience why lives were lost.

Abraham Lincoln served as the 16th president of the United States from 1860 until 1865. He is considered to be one of the country's greatest leaders.

*This drawing shows Lincoln delivering the Gettysburg Address.*

Four **score** and seven years ago our fathers brought forth on this continent a new nation, **conceived** in Liberty, and **dedicated** to the **proposition** that all men are created equal.
   Now we are engaged in a great civil war, testing whether that nation . . . can long **endure**. We are met on a great battle-field of that war. We have come to dedicate a portion of that field, as a final resting place for those who here gave their lives that that nation might live.

**Score** means twenty.
**Conceived** means thought up.
**Dedicated** means made for.
A **proposition** is an idea.
To **endure** means to last.

## Let's Compare

Speeches are often written during important times of change. Many are read as historical documents. However, they are not complete records of history.

Sarah E. Champion includes many details in *Our Flag*. She describes how "Washington drew with a pencil a design" and how Ross decided on the "five-pointed" star.

From Champion's book, readers are able to picture George Washington drawing a flag design and giving it to Betsy Ross to make into the first U.S. flag.

These details make her work a complete historical record.

Lincoln mentions "our fathers," "a new nation," "liberty," and "that all men are created equal." These words make Lincoln's audience think about the American Revolutionary War and the efforts people made then to win their freedom. Lincoln reminds his audience of this to persuade people to not give up fighting for the Union. Readers of the speech today can understand how uncertain our nation's future was in 1863.

## Nonfiction Writers

Shelley Tanaka has written nonfiction for children about knights, dinosaurs, mummies, disasters, ancient cultures, and remarkable people.

# Write Your Own Nonfiction

1. Share what matters. The best writing comes from a topic, or main subject, that means something to the writer.

2. Choose a style. Essays and reports are good choices for schoolwork. Keeping a diary is not only fun, but it is also great writing practice. Writing a postcard on vacation is a type of travel writing.

*Writing a postcard about your experiences is a type of nonfiction writing.*

3. If you need to know more about a topic, find the facts in books and on trusted websites. Encyclopedias are good resources to start with.

4. Let the words flow. Begin by writing down all the facts and thoughts you want to include. Don't worry about whether it sounds right or not. You can revise your writing later.

5. Be honest. Try writing as if you were simply telling a story to a friend.

6. Most important, have fun. Your readers are more likely to enjoy your writing if you do, too!

*Encyclopedias are reliable resources with facts about many topics.*

# GLOSSARY

**autobiography** A history of a person's life written by that person.

**biography** A history of a person's life written by another person.

**essay** A short piece of writing that expresses a writer's opinion on something.

**fiction** A made-up story that is not based on facts.

**journal** A record of what has happened; a diary.

**nonfiction** Writing based on real-life events, or true stories.

**poetry** Writing that uses patterns of sound, rhythm, or meaning to communicate ideas and feelings.

**report** Writing that explains or describes important ideas about a subject.

**rhythm** A pattern of beats or stressed sounds.

**speech** Writing meant to be spoken aloud to a specific audience.

**topic** Another word for "subject."

## Books

Fields, Jan. *You Can Write Excellent Reports*. Mankato, MN: First Facts Books, 2012.

Howell, Sara. *How to Write an Explanatory Text*. New York, NY: PowerKids Press, 2014.

Howell, Sara. *How to Write an Opinion Piece*. New York, NY: PowerKids Press, 2014.

Madden, Kerry, and Tracy McGuiness. *Writing Smarts: A Girl's Guide to Journaling, Poetry, Storytelling, and School Papers*. Middleton, WI: Pleasant Company Publications, 2002.

Tanaka, Shelley. *On Board the Titanic*. New York, NY: Hyperion, 1996.

Yolen, Jane. *Sea Queens: Women Pirates Around the World*. Watertown, MA: Charlesbridge Publishing, 2010 (reprint).

## Websites

Because of the changing nature of Internet links, Rosen Publishing has developed an online list of websites related to the subject of this book. This site is updated regularly. Please use this link to access this list:

http://www.rosenlinks.com/BCCL/Nonf

# INDEX